"DISCARD"

Witness History Series

THE RISE OF FASCISM

Peter Chrisp

The Bookwright Press
New York · 1991

Titles in this series

The Arab-Israeli Conflict
Blitzkrieg!
China since 1945
The Cold War
The Origins of World War I
The Rise of Fascism
The Russian Revolution
South Africa since 1948
The USSR under Stalin
The Third Reich
The United Nations
The United States since 1945
War in the Trenches

Cover illustration: An Italian magazine cover from the 1930s, showing Hitler and Mussolini in a typically fascist pose.

First published in the
United States in 1991 by
The Bookwright Press
387 Park Avenue South
New York, NY 10016

First published in 1991 by
Wayland (Publishers) Limited
61 Western Road, Hove
East Sussex BN3 1JD, England

© Copyright 1991 Wayland (Publishers) Limited

Library of Congress Cataloging-in-Publication Data
Chrisp, Peter.
    The rise of fascism / by Peter Chrisp.
       p. cm. – (Witness history series)
    Includes bibliographical references and index.
    Summary: Surveys the origins and causes of
European fascism, in such countries as Italy, Nazi
Germany, Spain, and Romania, and seeks common
characteristics of the different nationalistic fascist
movements.
    ISBN 0–531–18438–2
    1. Fascism – Europe – History – 20th century –
Juvenile literature.
    [1. Fascism – Europe – History.] I. Title. II. Series.
    D726.5.C48 1991
    320.5'33'094–dc20   90-46774
                                                                             CIP
                                                                             AC

Typeset by Kalligraphic Design Ltd, Horley, Surrey
Printed in Italy by G. Canale & C.S.p.A., Turin

Contents

1
ROOTS OF FASCISM
What is fascism?

T HE WORD "FASCIST" is very difficult to
define. It is used today as a term of abuse,
directed against people who believe that
strong government is more important than
individual freedom. But the word originally
referred to a specific political movement that
developed in Italy at the end of World War I.

The first fascist party was founded by
Benito Mussolini in 1919. Later, other political
movements that resembled Mussolini's were
also described as fascist. The most powerful
of these was Adolf Hitler's German Nazi
Party. Fascist Italy and Nazi Germany were
the only two true fascist regimes; but in many
other European countries political parties
were set up, inspired by Mussolini and Hitler.
They too have been called fascist.

One way of trying to understand fascism is
to look at the most important aims and
characteristics of the two fascist regimes and
other fascist parties. Fascism's most striking
characteristic was nationalism, the love of the
nation. Fascists reacted against the inter-
nationalism of communism. Communists
believed that the workers of all nations
should unite and recognize their common
interests. But the fascists thought that their
nations were better than all others. Their
nationalism was aggressive: fascist nations
would become great by conquering other,
weaker nations.

A second characteristic of fascism was its
aim of totalitarianism. The state was to have
total control over the lives of individual
citizens. Hitler and Mussolini believed that
there should be only one political party in the
state, and that it should control all sources of
information. Organizations were set up to
brainwash the young. There was constant
propaganda putting forward the party view.

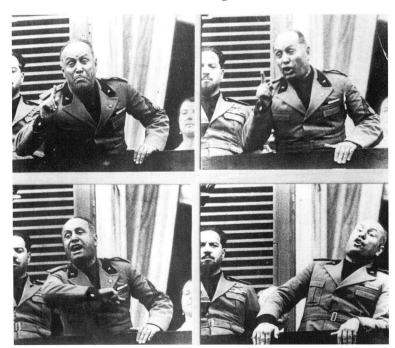

These stills from a newsreel
capture the Italian dictator
Mussolini in full flight.
Mussolini used theatrical skills –
dramatic pauses and violent
gestures – to win over his
audiences.

Opposing viewpoints were suppressed by censorship, and behind everything there was always the threat of arrest by a feared secret police force.

Related to fascism's totalitarianism was its militarism. The fascist parties, with their uniforms and parades, were closely modeled on the army, and they wanted to impose military values on the whole nation. Women were told that their role was to produce children for the nation's armies. War was glorified as a source of nobility and a sign of national health. The main fascist virtues were discipline and unquestioning obedience.

In the fascist state the ultimate source of authority was the leader – in Italy the Duce and in Germany the Führer. The fascist leaders owed their position to charisma, an intense personal spell with which they were able to sway their listeners. Propaganda presented them as wise figures who had been chosen by destiny as the nation's saviors. The devotion that they inspired could be religious in its intensity.

▲ The typical image of a fascist leader. Hitler, a figure of strength, grasps a banner on which is written "Loyalty," "Honor" and "Order." Germany, an idealized woman, clings to him for protection.

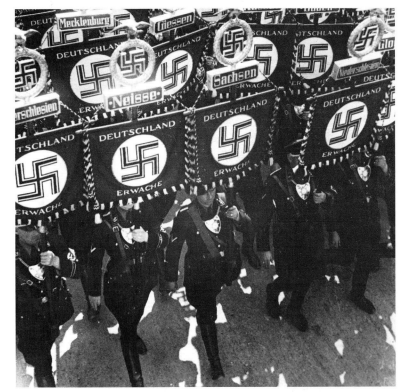

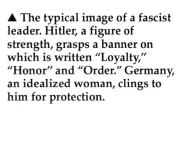

◀ SS guards parade at Nuremburg. Theatrically-staged military parades played a central role in fascism.

Where did fascist ideas come from?

Unlike modern communism, which is based on the writings of Karl Marx, there is no single source for the ideas of fascism. Mussolini himself wrote:

> Fascism was not the nursling of a doctrine worked out beforehand . . . it was born of a need for action and it was itself from the beginning practical rather than theoretical.[1]

What concerned Mussolini was the pursuit of power. He felt free to use and abandon political theories as they suited him. His main obsession, shared by all the fascist leaders, was the need for dynamic action. In Mussolini's case, a major inspiration was the French writer Georges Sorel (1847–1922).

Sorel was part of a political movement called syndicalism. The syndicalists were trade unionists who rejected parliamentary democracy; they called on the workers to seize power by direct action, in the form of a

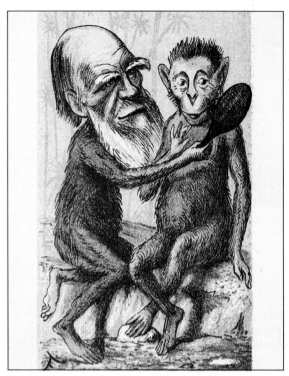

general strike. In his 1908 book, *Reflections on Violence*, Sorel praised the use of violent action and talked of the need for "myths" – ideas that would stir the masses into revolution. He argued that emotion rather than reason determined people's behavior. This rejection of reason in favor of "myths" was of major importance to Mussolini. In 1922, he proclaimed, "Our myth is the greatness of the nation!"[2]

Hitler held similar beliefs to those of Mussolini, but he drew his ideas from quite different sources. His most important influence was Social Darwinism. This was the application of the theories of the British scientist Charles Darwin (1809–82) to society. In *The Origin of Species* (1859), Darwin had presented life as a struggle for survival between different species. Those animals that

◀ In his book, *Mein Kampf*, Hitler set out his philosophy that the Germans were a "superior" race and had the right to conquer and enslave other, "inferior" races.

◀ Charles Darwin's theory that humans had evolved from apes was ridiculed when it was first published, but was later widely accepted. The Nazis distorted Darwin's theories, using them to justify warfare and racism.

▶ Friedrich Nietzsche despised democracy and Christian morality. He argued that Christian concern for the weak and the sick had corrupted civilization. Nietzsche prophesied the coming of a new kind of man, the "superman." The "superman" would be strong and hard, and would be able to invent his own rules of behavior. Both Mussolini and Hitler admired Nietzsche and saw themselves as "supermen."

are best adapted to their environment survive; the rest become extinct. Darwin's theory referred only to species of animals, but later writers applied it to different human races. Adolf Hitler explained:

> *Nature teaches us at every glance . . . that the strong is victorious and the weak is defeated . . . What appears cruel to man is self-evidently wise from the point of view of Nature. A nation that cannot maintain itself vanishes and another takes its place . . .* [3]

Traditional ideas of good and evil were scorned as sentimental nonsense.

Hitler was obsessed with the idea of life as a struggle, even calling his autobiography, *Mein Kampf (My Struggle)*. Social Darwinism played down the importance of the individual and the role of reason in decision making; people act the way they do because of heredity, race and environment.

The German philosopher Friedrich Nietzsche (1844–1900) provided another source for the rejection of reason and democracy. He also saw life as an eternal struggle, with victory going to the strong. What motivates people, he said, is the will to dominate others. He called for the rule of the "superman," the exceptional person who stood above normal morality.

The impact of World War I

Extreme nationalist movements existed in Europe before 1914. But it was World War I, which broke out in that year, that led to the rise of fascism. The war started as a European conflict between the Central Powers (Germany and Austria-Hungary) and the Allies (France, Belgium, Britain, Russia and Serbia). The Central Powers were then joined by Turkey and Bulgaria; the Allies by Japan, Italy, Romania, Portugal, Greece and the United States. There was fighting on a scale that had never been seen before, and it altered the character of Europe forever.

Before 1914, the dominant European

political belief had been liberalism, based on individual freedom and free trade among nations. However, World War I forced governments to take much more control over the lives of their citizens. Millions were conscripted into the war industries or armed forces. In place of trading freely with other nations, countries tried to become self-sufficient. Increased state control and economic self-sufficiency would later be the aims of the fascist regimes.

The war had a catastrophic effect in Russia, where heavy losses and economic chaos sparked off the communist revolution. In November 1917, the Bolshevik Party seized power and set up the first communist government in the world. The news of the

This map shows how many troops were mobilized and killed during World War I.

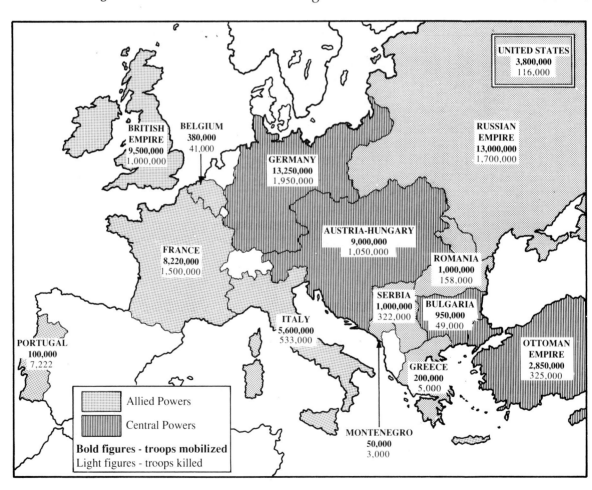

UNITED STATES
3,800,000
116,000

BRITISH EMPIRE
9,500,000
1,000,000

BELGIUM
380,000
41,000

GERMANY
13,250,000
1,950,000

RUSSIAN EMPIRE
13,000,000
1,700,000

FRANCE
8,220,000
1,500,000

AUSTRIA-HUNGARY
9,000,000
1,050,000

ROMANIA
1,000,000
158,000

SERBIA
1,000,000
322,000

BULGARIA
950,000
49,000

ITALY
5,600,000
533,000

PORTUGAL
100,000
7,222

GREECE
200,000
5,000

OTTOMAN EMPIRE
2,850,000
325,000

MONTENEGRO
50,000
3,000

Allied Powers

Central Powers

Bold figures - troops mobilized
Light figures - troops killed

Communists hoped that the Russian Revolution would quickly lead to a world revolution. Nikolai Kochergin's propaganda poster, "The First of May," shows the workers of all nations marching over the fallen symbols of monarchy and capitalism. Fear of the world revolution led many people to join the fascist parties.

Russian Revolution inspired communists throughout Europe, and there were uprisings in many countries, including Germany. Fear of communism was to be an important factor in the rise of fascism.

European governments had also encouraged the spread of patriotism as part of the war effort. The rise in nationalist feeling was bound to lead to disappointment when the war ended. In 1919, the victorious Allies redrew the map of Europe, setting up new countries at the expense of the defeated Central Powers. Disappointment was felt even on the winning side; Italians felt cheated by the peace settlement.

The greatest bitterness was felt by the returning soldiers. After years at the front they returned home expecting a hero's welcome, to be met instead by the prospect of unemployment. As war industries shut down, thousands of workers were unemployed and no one knew what to do with the demobilized soldiers. Many workers turned to communism as an answer to economic crisis. However, some soldiers who had spent years in an atmosphere of patriotic propaganda and organized violence were attracted to the new fascist parties. One ex-soldier who joined the Nazi Party explained:

The war had taught us one lesson, the great community of the front. All class differences disappeared under its spell. There was only one people, no individuals. Common suffering and a common peril had welded us together.[4]

With its nationalist fervor, fascism appealed to patriotic soldiers far more than communism.

2

FASCIST ITALY
Italy and World War I

This Italian cartoon makes fun of pretended friendship between a Socialist (in red) and a Fascist. At first the two parties seemed to have much in common, but they soon became bitter enemies.

AT THE OUTBREAK of World War I, Italy was politically and economically backward. The country was not unified completely until 1870, and even then the powerful Roman Catholic Church refused to recognize the new Italian state. Until 1903, it forbade Catholics to participate in elections. While the north of Italy was beginning to be industrialized, the south was a land of poor, illiterate peasants. It was not until 1912 that all men over thirty were given the vote. The parliamentary system was ineffective and widely regarded as corrupt. Government ministries changed frequently; there were thirty-one between 1860 and 1914.

A country as unstable as Italy was ill-prepared to fight in a major world war. But in 1915, lured by Allied promises of territory,

Italy declared war on Austria. In 1917, the Italian army was decisively defeated at Caporetto, and was saved only by swift Allied help in the form of troops and supplies.

Although Italy was on the victorious side, the war created a political and economic crisis. The cost of the war had been enormous, and with the ending of Allied financial help, the economy was close to collapse. The closing of munitions factories and the demobilization of thousands of soldiers created massive unemployment. Faced with soaring inflation and low wages, the trade unions organized a wave of sit-down strikes. In the south, peasants began to take over the great estates. Inspired by the Bolsheviks, the growing Socialist Party called for power to be handed to workers' and peasants' councils. Italy seemed on the brink of revolution.

Italians also felt cheated by the peace treaties. The Allies had promised Italy the territories of South Tyrol, Istria with the port of Fiume and Dalmatia. But in 1919, Dalmatia was given to the newly created Yugoslavia, and Fiume was to be governed by an international commission. Italy's gains – Istria and the South Tyrol – seemed small compensation for the half a million Italians who had died in the war.

In September 1919, the poet Gabriele D'Annunzio marched into Fiume with a thousand followers, mainly demobilized soldiers, and declared that the port was annexed to Italy. His men wore black shirts decorated with a skull and crossbones, and saluted in "Roman fashion" by stiffly raising their arms. D'Annunzio would address them from a balcony, and they would reply with chants ("Italy or death!") and rhythmic cries ("Ayah, ayah, alala!"). After fifteen months Yugoslavia and Italy agreed that Fiume should be independent, and D'Annunzio was driven out. But he had created the style of fascism.

Gabriele D'Annunzio, the patriotic poet, became an Italian national hero when he led a private army into Fiume.

Mussolini and the *Fasci di Combattimento*

Before the war, Benito Mussolini had been a leading figure in the revolutionary wing of the Socialist Party and had edited the party newspaper, *Avanti!*, in Milan. The Socialist Party was internationalist, and it opposed Italy's entry into the war, a position Mussolini at first supported. But in November 1914, he underwent an abrupt and unexpected change of attitude. In a new paper, *Il Popolo d'Italia*, he called for Italian intervention, claiming that war would lead to revolution. He was expelled from the party as a traitor.

Italy was deeply divided over intervention. The Church and the Socialists

Members of the Fascist Militia – the party's private army – assemble for a massive rally in Naples, October 24, 1922.

wanted peace, and most workers and peasants supported them. As an interventionist, Mussolini found himself allied to nationalists, financiers, some syndicalists (revolutionary trade unionists) and other unorthodox socialists. Soon after Italy entered the war Mussolini was drafted, spending several months at the front before being wounded. Back in Milan, he claimed to speak for Italy's soldiers: "We, the survivors . . . demand the right of governing Italy."[5]

In the revolutionary atmosphere of 1919, Mussolini saw an opportunity to build a new political movement based on the returning soldiers. In March, he declared the formation of *Fasci di Combattimento* (Combat Groups). The Fascists were to be revolutionary, but unlike the Socialists they would also be

nationalistic. At first, Mussolini hoped to win over the working classes, defending strikes and calling for improved working conditions. But he failed to win any significant support from the workers, who remained loyal to the Socialist Party, or from the peasants, who followed the new Catholic Popular Party. In the November elections, the Fascists could not win a single seat.

Mussolini was not deterred, however. His earliest followers were mainly discontented ex-soldiers, to whom violence came easily. They attacked Socialists and burned down their newspaper offices. After August 1920, when trade unions organized a mass occupation of the factories, the Fascists began to act as strikebreakers. Their blackshirted squads would beat up militant workers and peasants. The army provided them with weapons, and the police did not intervene – a pattern that was to be repeated again and again. Mussolini also began to receive support from industrialists and landowners, who saw the Fascists as the only force tough enough to beat the "reds."

The Liberal prime minister, Giolitti, hoped to use the Fascists as a counterbalance against the working-class parties, the Socialists and the Catholic Popular Party. In 1921, he invited Mussolini to join a "national bloc" of government parties. Thanks to government support, in May 1921 Mussolini and thirty-five Fascists were elected to parliament. Giolitti expected to turn the Fascists into a respectable parliamentary party.

▲ Giovanni Giolitti, the Liberal prime minister, believed he could tame fascism.

◀ Mussolini's *Il Popolo d'Italia* was originally subtitled "a socialist newspaper." But following his break with the Socialists, the subtitle was changed to "the newspaper of combatants and producers." In this September 1919 edition, he denounces the government for failing to support D'Annunzio's occupation of Fiume, and demands the resignation of Prime Minister Nitti.

The march on Rome

Once elected, Mussolini refused to support Giolitti, whose government swiftly fell. Giolitti's successors, Bonomi (1921-2) and Facta (1922), were even less effective in producing a stable government. This weakness was shown in August 1922, when the Socialists proclaimed a general strike in protest against Fascist violence. While the government did nothing, it took the Fascists themselves a single day to smash the strike. Fascism increasingly seemed to be the only alternative force to socialism.

In September 1922, Mussolini negotiated with Facta to bring the Fascists into a coalition government. Meanwhile he was under increasing pressure from his own radical followers to seize power. Italo Balbo, the Fascist *ras* (chief) of Ferrara, and Roberto Farinacci, the *ras* of Cremona, had established their own local regimes, often acting independently of Mussolini. As the government crisis deepened, Balbo and the radicals began to talk of a march on Rome. For a while Mussolini restrained the radicals, but on October 24 he told a mass Fascist rally in Naples, "Either they give us the government or we go to Rome and take it."[6]

Four days later, approximately 28,000 Fascists gathered outside Rome. Facta's government, which had tolerated Fascist violence for months, finally decided to act, declaring martial law. But King Victor

Italo Balbo was the Fascist *ras* (chief) of Ferrara, where he organized the blackshirts into a military force. Throughout the summer of 1922, he led his squads through the provinces of Ferrara and Ravenna, attacking Socialists and trade unionists and burning down their buildings. Balbo's campaigns showed how completely state authority and the rule of law had broken down.

Mussolini was invited to form a government twenty-four hours before the Fascists entered Rome. The "march on Rome," shown in this photograph, was really a victory parade.

Emmanuel refused to sign the proclamation. On October 29, without a shot being fired, the king invited Mussolini to form his own government. The heavily-armed garrison of Rome could easily have defeated the poorly-armed blackshirts. But the king had a number of reasons for holding back.

To fire on the Fascists might have resulted in a civil war, leading to a left-wing revolution. In any case, the king could not be sure of the loyalty of the army, which had been helping the Fascists for months. Six generals actually took part in the march on Rome, and the military had even misled the king, telling him that there were 100,000 Fascists outside the city. His position was also weakened by the claim to the throne of his ambitious cousin, the pro-Fascist Duke of Aosta. On September 20, Mussolini had

offered his support to the monarchy if it did nothing to oppose the "Fascist revolution."[7] The threat was clear.

Facta's weak government was simply too discredited to find any effective defenders. The heads of industry had telegraphed Rome, asking for Mussolini to be made prime minister. One industrialist later remembered:

We did not want dictatorship; all we wanted was simply that Mussolini, when he took over the government, should bring back order and tranquillity to the country. After that, we would have gone back to the old system.[8]

This was not a realistic expectation.

Toward dictatorship 1922–5

Mussolini was prime minister, but the Fascists still had only thirty-five seats in parliament. His first cabinet was a coalition, drawing on all the anti-socialist parties. In order to win a Fascist majority, Mussolini persuaded parliament to change the electoral system. Under the new method, the party or bloc gaining the majority of votes would automatically get two-thirds of the seats. The Socialists opposed the measure, while the

Catholic Popular Party abstained. But the Liberals gave Mussolini their support. They hoped that a Fascist majority would strengthen Mussolini against his radical followers, who were talking of doing away with parliament altogether.

In the April 1924 election, the Fascist-Liberal bloc obtained four and a half million votes (64 percent). Many middle-class people, reassured by the ending of the strikes, voted for the strong government that Mussolini represented. But the size of the victory was due to electoral corruption. Blackshirts

Mussolini's aggressive style of oratory is captured in this photograph of him speaking in Rome.

This socialist cartoon from the satirical paper, *Il Becco Giallo*, links Mussolini with the murder of Matteotti. Once Mussolini had successfully consolidated his power, all such criticism was banned.

prevented other parties from campaigning and tampered with ballot boxes.

Hopes that Fascism might be tamed were soon disappointed. On May 30 the Socialist deputy Giacomo Matteotti, an outspoken critic of Mussolini, made a speech demanding that the elections be declared invalid. Eleven days later he was kidnapped and murdered, though his body was not found until August. Matteotti had already been savagely beaten on several occasions by blackshirts, so they were the obvious suspects. Angry crowds gathered below Mussolini's windows, demanding Matteotti's body. The opposition deputies withdrew from parliament in moral protest. For several days it looked as if the government might fall. But the Liberals, the industrialists and the king continued to back Mussolini, fearing a revival of socialism – though they also put him under increasing pressure to curb the undisciplined blackshirts.

At first Mussolini seemed willing to compromise. But he was also under pressure from the radical Fascists, hostile to any concessions. On December 31, several thousand Fascists held a rally in Florence and carried the following motion:

> *The Florentine Fascists . . . declare their loyalty to the Duce . . . but make their obedience and their discipline conditional on the decisive action of the government, which must be demonstrated, if necessary, by dictatorial action.*[9]

The Fascists wanted all or nothing.

Three days later, Mussolini made a fiery speech in parliament, in which he assumed full responsibility for the blackshirts' actions. "Force is the only solution!" he cried.[10] Within hours the Fascist militia, the party's private army, was mobilized. Opposition newspapers were confiscated and opponents were arrested. Mussolini had declared himself dictator of Italy.

Over the following months, Mussolini issued a series of decrees dissolving the other political parties and ending free elections. Newspapers were brought under Fascist control or suppressed. With the opposition destroyed, Mussolini could now start to build a Fascist state. What would it be like?

The Fascist state

After 1926, Mussolini began to talk about "the corporative state." This was the Fascist solution to the problem of industrial conflict. It was based on the idea that the interests of individuals or classes should be set aside for the greater good of the nation.

In each area of the economy a corporation was set up that would include both employers' and workers' organizations. Strikes were banned but so were lock-outs by employers. Disputes would be solved by a Fascist labor court. In Italy and abroad this system was praised as an alternative to both capitalism and communism. But in practice the arrangement favored the employers, who were able to choose their own representatives, while representatives of the workers were appointed by the state. Without bargaining power, workers had to accept an 11 percent cut in real wages between the years 1925 and 1938.

How do you make people put their nation above private interests? Mussolini talked of creating a new kind of Italian, who would be molded by military discipline like the soldiers of ancient Rome. Education was brought under the control of the Fascist Party, and the Roman Empire took a central place in history courses.

Each school day would start with the singing of the Fascist anthem, *Giovinezza* ("Youth"). Then the children would march past the flag, giving the Roman salute. At the age of four, boys were encouraged to join the "Sons of the She-Wolf," a Fascist youth organization. At eight, they would move on to the *Balilla*. Blackshirted *Balilla* boys would drill with toy guns and learn Fascist slogans: "Mussolini is always right," "Believe! Obey! Fight!," "A minute on the battlefield is worth a lifetime of peace" and "Better to live one day like a lion than a hundred years as a sheep." Girls also had their organizations, the *Piccole Italiane* and the female *Balilla*. They took part in sports activities, but they were taught that a woman's place was in the home, bringing up children.

Propaganda played a major role in winning over the Italian people. Mussolini said that the Italian nation was in a "permanent state of war."[11] Every issue was presented as a battle. There was a "Battle for Births" to encourage people to have more children, and a "Battle for Grain" to make Italy self-sufficient in food.

BENITO MUSSOLINI

ama molto i bambini.

I bimbi d'Italia amano

molto il Duce.

VIVA IL DUCE!

Saluto al Duce:

A noi!

Fascist propaganda was even aimed at very young children. The text on this poster reads: "Benito Mussolini loves children very much. The children of Italy love the Duce very much. Long live the Duce: To us!" Pictures such as this one decorated every schoolroom.

A.IX
ERA FASCISTA
ANNO 1:- N: 28
·27 SETTEMBRE

**The cover of the magazine,
Fascist Youth, dated "Year Nine
of the Fascist Era" (1931).**

Central to Fascist propaganda was the cult of *Il Duce*. Mussolini was presented as a godlike figure whose eyes were on everyone and who knew everything that happened in Italy. His official biography told Italians that the Duce was regarded throughout the world as the greatest genius alive. The lights of his office were left on at night to show how hard he worked. At the same time, he was presented as a man of action. He was photographed helping with the harvest, stripped to the waist, or jogging along the beach in his bathing trunks. Mussolini's love of car racing, horse riding, fencing and flying was well publicized. When his fourth child was born, propaganda hailed "the confirmed proof of a virility that is a model for all Italians."[12] But the press was not allowed to report that he was ill with a stomach ulcer, or that he had become a grandfather. Mussolini

had to appear young and fit. In a 1932 interview with a German journalist, Emil Ludwig, the Duce explained his relationship with the Italian people:

> *For me the masses are nothing but a herd of sheep as long as they are unorganized . . . The Roman greeting, songs and formulas . . . all are essential to fan the flames of the enthusiasm that keeps a movement in being . . . It is faith that moves mountains, not reason. Reason is a tool, but it can never be the motive force of the crowd . . . Everything turns upon one's ability to control the masses like an artist.*[13]

The Italians were supposed to believe in Mussolini. He would never have revealed his contempt like this to an Italian journalist.

A totalitarian state?

Mussolini described totalitarianism as "Everything within the State, nothing outside the State, nothing against the State."[14] One of the first institutions to be brought under centralized state control was the Fascist Party itself. In the struggle for power, Mussolini had had difficulty in controlling his more radical followers. During 1927–8, he imposed strict discipline on the party. Its list of candidates would now be presented from above rather than chosen locally. In this way he broke the strength of the independent *ras* (chiefs), whose positions relied on their local following.

After 1932, Mussolini also encouraged mass membership in the party. A party card was necessary to get any job connected with the state, so thousands joined. In the process

To make his soldiers more aggressive, Mussolini made them adopt the German goose step. He claimed it was the marching step of ancient Rome.

the Fascist Party lost its special status and its political role. Policy was determined by Mussolini alone. By increasing his own powers, he prevented the emergence of a ruling élite that might eventually challenge him. "Fascism," he declared, "is Mussolinism."[15] On another occasion he said, "My successor has not yet been born."[16] Mussolini's attitudes did nothing to provide for the stability of his regime or its survival in the event of his death.

There were also strong forces working against Mussolini's ideal of a totalitarian state. Two important institutions still commanded loyalty independently of the Duce: the monarchy and the Church.

Unlike Hitler, Mussolini never took on all the powers of the head of state. King Victor Emmanuel, although deeply implicated in the Fascist regime, could also become the focus for opposition to Mussolini; he could

still command some loyalty from the army, for instance.

To appease the Church, in 1929, Mussolini accepted Catholicism as the state religion and became a practicing Catholic, despite the fact that he had once written a pamphlet called *God Does Not Exist*. In return, the Pope recognized the Italian state. This reconciliation with the Church has been described as Mussolini's greatest achievement. Yet the Church remained an important rival to fascism, another movement based on faith. Catholic youth organizations competed with the Fascists in an attempt to capture the souls of the people.

The aim of totalitarianism was further undermined by the inefficiency of the regime. The functions of the Fascist Party, the civil service and the corporations often overlapped, and Mussolini encouraged rivalry between them. To increase his own power, he followed a policy of "divide and rule." But in the resulting confusion, his orders were often lost or deliberately mislaid. One party secretary described him as "the most disobeyed man in history."[17] Despite his image as a man of action, he was frequently indecisive. Senior officials said that his was a "dictatorship of soft cheese."[18]

3

NAZI GERMANY
The Weimar Republic

IN OCTOBER 1918, after four years of war, the German navy mutinied and a wave of anti-war strikes spread throughout the country. Following the Soviet example, workers, soldiers and sailors set up revolutionary councils to seize power. On November 9, with the country in chaos, the Kaiser (emperor) abdicated and a Republic was proclaimed. Two days later the new government signed an armistice that brought the war to an end. Many patriotic Germans saw this act as a terrible betrayal. The German army had not been defeated in battle, they said, but stabbed in the back by the "November criminals" – the politicians who set up the new Weimar Republic.

The country's new rulers claimed that only a democratic Germany could hope for a just peace with the Allies. But in 1919, the victorious nations forced Germany to sign the Treaty of Versailles. In order to justify their own involvement in the war, British and French governments had to blame and punish the Germans. Under the terms of the peace treaty, Germany lost large areas of territory to neighboring countries, had its

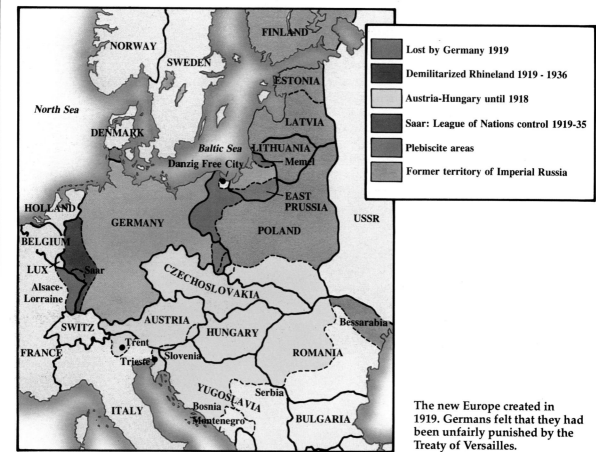

	Lost by Germany 1919
	Demilitarized Rhineland 1919 - 1936
	Austria-Hungary until 1918
	Saar: League of Nations control 1919-35
	Plebiscite areas
	Former territory of Imperial Russia

The new Europe created in 1919. Germans felt that they had been unfairly punished by the Treaty of Versailles.

◀ Units of the Bavarian *Freikorps*, in traditional costume, march through Munich on May 1, 1919, during the suppression of the short-lived Soviet Republic. They killed 700 people, many of them non-Communists, in revenge for the shooting of twelve hostages by the Republic.

▼ French troops occupy the Ruhr in January 1923. This was yet another humiliation for Germany.

army reduced to 100,000 men, and was made to accept the responsibility for having started the war. Germany also had to pay enormous sums in reparation (compensation) for the damage caused by the war. This treaty reinforced the German people's growing lack of support for the new democracy.

The new government was a coalition of the Social Democratic Party (moderate socialists), the Catholic Center Party and the Democratic Party. At first the greatest danger to this government came from the revolutionary communists and socialists. In January 1919, there was the communist "Spartacus Revolt" in Berlin. The following month, a Soviet Republic was proclaimed in Munich, the capital of Bavaria. To restore order, the government was forced to rely on volunteer units of patriotic ex-soldiers, the *Freikorps* (free corps). On their return from the front, these men had been horrified to find the red flag flying in the place of the imperial colors. The *Freikorps* brutally crushed the communist risings. But that did not mean they had any allegiance to the new democratic Republic.

The Republic was also threatened by economic crisis. Weakened by the war, Germany's economy now had the additional burden of reparations payments. In January 1923, when the government failed to pay reparations, French troops occupied Germany's most important industrial area, the Ruhr. The government called for passive resistance, and the miners and steelworkers of the Ruhr went on strike.

The Ruhr occupation only deepened the economic crisis and forced the government to print more paper money to keep the economy functioning. With more money in circulation, its value fell rapidly. Inflation, already rising, now ran out of control. In a few months, Germany's middle classes saw the value of their life savings wiped out.

Hitler and the Nazi Party 1919–23

After the suppression of the Bavarian Soviet Republic, Bavaria became a center for right-wing opposition to the Berlin government. One of the Munich groups was the tiny German Workers' Party, a nationalist organization that blamed Jews for all of Germany's misfortunes. Jews had been prominent among the leaders of the communists. Communism was also opposed to nationalism and the Jews were an international race. So it was easy, though completely untrue, to say that communism itself was Jewish.

Adolf Hitler had spent the war as a Lance-Corporal in a Bavarian infantry regiment. When he returned to Munich he continued to work for the army as a propaganda officer, counteracting the spread of communism among the soldiers. In September 1919, he was sent to investigate the German Workers' Party. Impressed by their ideas, he became a member. Hitler had a domineering personality and was a powerful public speaker. During 1920 – 21, he became the undisputed leader of the party, which was renamed the National Socialist German Workers' Party (shortened to Nazi Party).

The Nazi program included socialist measures to win over the workers; Nazis wanted the nationalization of big businesses and the abolition of unearned incomes. But its main demand was for the union of all Germans, excluding German Jews, in a Greater Germany (*Großdeutschland*). There was also a Nazi paramilitary wing, called the *Sturmabteilung* (storm-troopers), or SA. Storm-troopers beat up hecklers at Nazi meetings and fought street battles with the communists.

In 1923, the Ruhr occupation and hyperinflation encouraged the enemies of the Weimar Republic to plot the government's downfall. There were communist uprisings in Saxony, Thuringia and Hamburg. Inspired by the success of Mussolini's march on Rome, right-wing Bavarians began to talk of retaliation with a march on "Red Berlin." The right-wing group included members of

The collapse of the mark. Because of hyperinflation, in July 1923 clerks needed huge baskets to collect paper money from the Reichsbank for the payment of wages. Soon even these baskets would be too small.

the Bavarian government and army, monarchists, Bavarian separatists and the Nazis. These people all had widely differing aims, and were united only by their hatred of the Republic.

However, by November, the Berlin government was reasserting its authority, and the German army was used to suppress the communist uprisings. Hitler's allies in the Bavarian government now felt less enthusiastic about the march on Berlin. On November 8–9, to force the issue, the Nazis took over a meeting being held in a beer hall by the Bavarian leaders. At gunpoint, Hitler proclaimed a national revolution, or *Putsch*.

Hitler (second left) with right-wing Bavarians, two months before his failed *Putsch*.

The Bavarian politicians went along with Hitler at first, but when they were allowed to leave the beer hall they promptly denounced him and called out the police and army. The following day, the Nazis were scattered by police gunfire as they marched through Munich. Hitler was arrested and imprisoned. The *Putsch* failed because, unlike the case in Italy, the police and the army remained loyal to the state. But failure taught Hitler an important lesson. From now on he would follow the parliamentary path to power.

Nazism becomes a mass movement

Fascist movements thrive on crisis, but the second half of the 1920s was a period of political stability. Under the American Dawes Plan, reparation payments were reduced and the German economy was propped up by loans from the United States. Hitler was a forgotten man. It was not until 1929 that a fresh crisis gave him another opportunity.

The Wall Street Crash, a collapse of share values on the New York Stock Exchange, led to a sharp decline in world trading. The American banks called in their foreign loans. German industry, deprived of its export market and its American investment, was forced to lay off millions of workers.

Unemployment figures in Germany

January 1928	1,862,000
January 1929	2,850,000
January 1930	3,217,000
January 1931	4,886,000
January 1932	6,042,000

The government coalition of democratic parties broke up, unable to agree on a solution to the unemployment. From 1930 onward, Germany was governed by a succession of chancellors who had little parliamentary support; they were appointed from above by the head of state, President von Hindenburg. When these chancellors were forced to rule by emergency decree, it seemed that the democratic system had stopped working. But unemployment continued to rise.

Meanwhile, the Nazis were growing in strength. The SA recruited an army of 300,000 men, more than 60 percent of them unemployed. Party membership rose from 178,000 in 1929 to 800,000 in 1931. But most spectacular was the rise in electoral support, shown on the chart opposite.

A major reason for this spectacular success was the skill of Nazi propaganda. It was specifically tailored for different groups: when Hitler spoke to industrialists or to a middle-class audience he stressed the threat of communism; when he spoke to the unemployed he promised bread and work. The German people's frustration and resentment were directed against easy targets, the Jews and the "November criminals." But at the same time Hitler also presented what appeared to be a positive message. After a 1932 Hamburg mass meeting addressed by Hitler, a schoolteacher named Luise Solmitz wrote in her diary:

How many look up to Hitler with touching faith, as their helper, their savior, their deliverer from unbearable distress – to Hitler, who rescues the Prussian prince, the scholar, the clergyman, the farmer, the worker, the unemployed – to Hitler who rescues them from the parties back into the nation.[19]

"We will accept any reasonable offer," announces the notice in this small store, forced to sell out by the depression. Owners of small stores felt threatened by big business and by communism – the Nazi Party seemed to provide the answer to their problems.

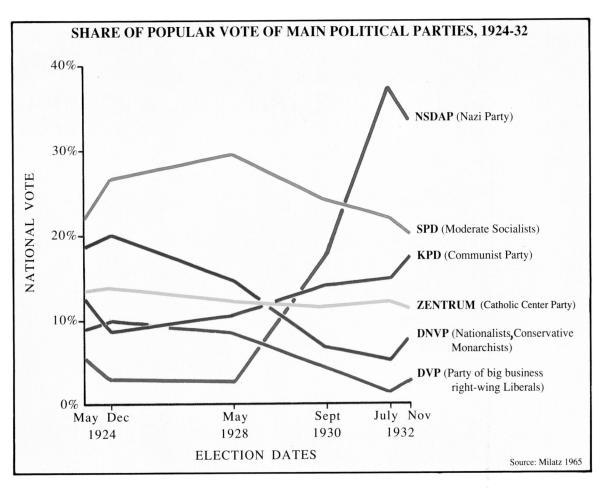

SHARE OF POPULAR VOTE OF MAIN POLITICAL PARTIES, 1924-32

NATIONAL VOTE

40%

30%

20%

10%

0%

NSDAP (Nazi Party)

SPD (Moderate Socialists)

KPD (Communist Party)

ZENTRUM (Catholic Center Party)

DNVP (Nationalists, Conservative Monarchists)

DVP (Party of big business right-wing Liberals)

May Dec
1924

May
1928

Sept
1930

July Nov
1932

ELECTION DATES

Source: Milatz 1965

▲ This chart shows the Nazis' dramatic rise in popularity during the depression.

▶ "Germany lives!" is the message of this poster, showing Hitler as a savior, leading his troops to a brighter future.

With its doctrine of class warfare, Communist propaganda could appeal to only one social group, the working class. But Hitler's nationalism could reach across class barriers and give people a sense that they belonged to a single community. Hitler's attraction was that he claimed to stand above party politics. Many Germans were disillusioned with the warring parties and with a failing democracy. Unlike other German politicians, Hitler seemed to offer them strong leadership.

Hitler in power

▲ "The Marshal and the Lance-Corporal. Fight with Us for Peace and Rights." The aging President von Hindenburg was used to give legitimacy to the new regime.

By 1932, the Nazis were the largest party in the Reichstag (parliament) and the government could no longer ignore their claims. The chancellor, Franz von Papen, invited Hitler to join a coalition with the Nationalists. But Hitler refused, demanding to be made chancellor himself. After months of intrigue, von Papen persuaded Hindenburg to appoint Hitler chancellor in a coalition government. Warned of the danger of this move, von Papen replied, "You are wrong. We have hired him."[20] Only three of the twelve cabinet posts would be occupied by Nazis. Like the Italian Liberals ten years previously, von Papen believed he could tame and absorb fascism.

On January 30, 1933, Hitler became chancellor. His first act was to announce new elections, to be held in March. On the eve of the elections the Reichstag was set on fire. A lone Dutch Communist, Marinus van der Lubbe, was arrested in the burning building and confessed (though many people suspected the Nazis themselves of having started the fire). The fire gave Hitler an excuse to order the arrest of thousands of prominent Communists and socialists. An emergency decree was passed immediately abolishing

▶ The burning of Germany's parliament, the Reichstag, was blamed on the communists. It gave Hitler an excuse to crush his enemies.

THEY SALUTE WITH BOTH HANDS NOW.

the freedom of the press and the right to hold public meetings.

The March election took place in an atmosphere of terror, with only the Nazis and Nationalists able to campaign freely. Nonetheless the two parties achieved only a 52 percent majority. When the new assembly met, the building was surrounded by SA men. Communists and many Social Democrats were prevented from taking their seats. Hitler persuaded the assembly to pass an Enabling Act, giving him dictatorial powers for a period of four years.

The Nazis were now the rulers of Germany and could consolidate their power stage by stage. Over the next few months the other political parties were abolished or forced to dissolve; trade unions were banned and replaced by a new German Labor Front; and the independent state governments were brought under Nazi control.

The only threat to Hitler's position came from his own radical followers, the

A British cartoon commenting on the "Night of the Long Knives." Hitler, Goering and Goebbels, supported by the army, arrest the brownshirts. There would be no place for undisciplined revolutionaries in Hitler's new state.

brownshirted SA. Like Mussolini, Hitler had made use of violent revolutionaries in the struggle for power, but found no place for them in his new state. He wanted to win the support of the army, which saw the SA as a dangerous rival, and of Germany's industrialists, who feared the SA's revolutionary demands. For their part, the discontented SA leadership began to talk of a "second revolution" against the conservatives who now surrounded Hitler. On June 30, 1934, Hitler ordered his élite force, the *Schutzstaffel*, or SS, to arrest and shoot SA leaders. Hundreds of Nazis were murdered in what became known as the "Night of the Long Knives." Soon after, the army showed its gratitude by swearing an oath of allegiance to Hitler.

The Nazi state

Nazi Germany had a number of similarities with Fascist Italy. Like Mussolini, Hitler tried to make his country economically self-sufficient. He brought education under Nazi control and set up organizations to win over Germany's youth. Mussolini would have approved of Hitler's description of the role of women:

> *The woman has her own battlefield. With every child that she brings into the world, she fights her battle for the nation.*[21]

Even the need to produce new little fascists was presented as a call to arms.

The Nazis also swamped Germany with constant propaganda. Joseph Goebbels, the minister for propaganda, explained its importance:

> *It is not enough to reconcile people more or less to our regime, to move them towards a position of neutrality towards us, we want rather to work on people until they are addicted to us.*[22]

"The German Student Fights for Führer and People." The idealized German youth is blond, fit and wearing a uniform. Like the Italian Fascists, the Nazis were particularly concerned with winning over the young.

This quotation explains an essential difference between the fascist regimes and previous dictatorships. Before fascism, authoritarian regimes wanted only to destroy opposition. This was not enough for the fascists. The people of Nazi Germany and Fascist Italy were also expected to show constant enthusiasm for their rulers. Germans were expected to hang swastika flags from their windows and to greet each other by saying *"Heil Hitler."* People who criticized the Nazis ran the risk of being denounced to the Gestapo, the secret police. Children were encouraged to spy on their parents, and adults to keep watch on their neighbors. Leisure time was organized through the Nazi "Strength Through Joy" vacations. Robert Ley, head of the German Labor Front, boasted:

The only people who still have a private life in Germany are those who are asleep.[23]

Mussolini must have envied this boast.

An exhibition of German youth and fitness, from the 1935 Nuremburg rally.

These characteristics of Nazi Germany were all shared by Fascist Italy, but to a lesser extent; the Germans were far more efficient than the Italians in controlling the lives of ordinary citizens. Some historians claim that this is due to differences in "national character." Unlike the Italians, Germans already had a long tradition of militarism and of obedience to authority.

But the Italians did not share one important aspect of Nazi rule – the Nazis' obsession with race. Hitler believed that the Germans were the "master race," with the right to enslave "inferior" races and the duty to remain racially "pure." In practice, Nazis persecuted the Jews. Jews were deprived of their German citizenship, forbidden to marry other Germans, excluded from most jobs and banned from many public places. The persecution of the Jews grew progressively worse throughout the 1930s, eventually leading to the systematic murder of six million people during World War II.

Internal conflict

Hitler was much more successful than Mussolini in creating a totalitarian system. But if we look beyond the image of the all-powerful German state, we find many of the same contradictions and tensions that existed in Italy. Albert Speer, the Nazi armaments minister, described Hitler's style of government:

> He ... did not like establishing clear lines of jurisdiction. Sometimes he deliberately assigned bureaus or individuals the same or similar tasks. "That way," he used to say, "the stronger one does the job." [24]

Did Hitler act in this way because he viewed life as a constant struggle, with victory going to the strongest? Or was he encouraging rivalry to protect his own authority? Whatever the reason, the result was administrative confusion. The Civil Service, the ministries, the Nazi Party, the SS and the army were in constant conflict over their overlapping areas of authority. The only unifying factor was their loyalty to Hitler. But he was not interested in domestic policy and was impatient with administrative details, so the rival institutions were allowed great freedom to improvise policies and to increase their own spheres of influence.

Historians disagree over how far Hitler was in control of this system or how much it developed through its own momentum. An American historian, Norman Rich, says that "Hitler was master in the Third Reich." [25] But a German historian, Hans Mommsen, writes:

> [Hitler was] unwilling to take decisions, frequently uncertain, exclusively concerned with upholding his prestige and personal authority, influenced in the strongest fashion by his current entourage, in some respects a weak dictator. [26]

Perhaps in some ways Hitler was a "weak dictator," but his ability to maintain his personal authority and the way in which he held the different factions together could be seen as a sign of strength. As in Italy, the overriding importance of the leader

This Nazi children's book contrasts the blond "Aryan" who "can work and fight" with the Jew, "the greatest scoundrel in the whole Reich."

undermined the long-term stability of the regime. Many historians have been led to wonder what would have happened to Nazi Germany without Hitler.

The unity of Nazi Germany depended in part on the existence of enemies, both inside and outside the nation. The Nazis had come to power by stressing the threat from the communists, and they continued to need enemies to provide them with a sense of purpose. First the Jews, then gypsies, homosexuals and other nonconformists were persecuted. These people were called community aliens who threatened the great "folk community" by their very existence.

Hitler inspects a regiment of the *Schutzstaffel*, or SS. The SS began life as Hitler's own personal bodyguard, but gradually the organization increased its power and influence until it could interfere in almost every area of life in Nazi Germany.

The external enemy was described as "international Jewry"; rather illogically, Jews were presented as the secret driving power behind both the Western democracies and the USSR. Nazi institutions were also given a common purpose by the drive toward rearmament and war. Foreign conquests would allow them the scope to increase their own administrative empires.

4

THE SPANISH CIVIL WAR
A divided nation

BETWEEN 1936 AND 1939, Spain was split apart by a bloody civil war. On one side were the forces of a democratically elected Republic, on the other the right-wing forces of General Francisco Franco. This war has often been described as a conflict between democracy and fascism, a rehearsal for World War II. Franco received troops and money from Mussolini and Hitler. From all over Europe, workers and intellectuals volunteered to go to Spain to fight for the Republic. The British socialist writer George Orwell spoke for all of them when he said that he went to Spain "to fight against Fascism."[27]

The war was really the result of many complex forces.

In the 1930s, Spain was a poor and backward nation with few large cities. The little modern industry was concentrated in Catalonia and the Basque Provinces, in the northeast of the country. Many Spaniards were peasants or small farmers, conservative and strongly influenced by the Catholic Church. However, many other people were eager for change.

In the south, the province of Andalusia was inhabited largely by landless peasants. They worked for tiny wages as day laborers on

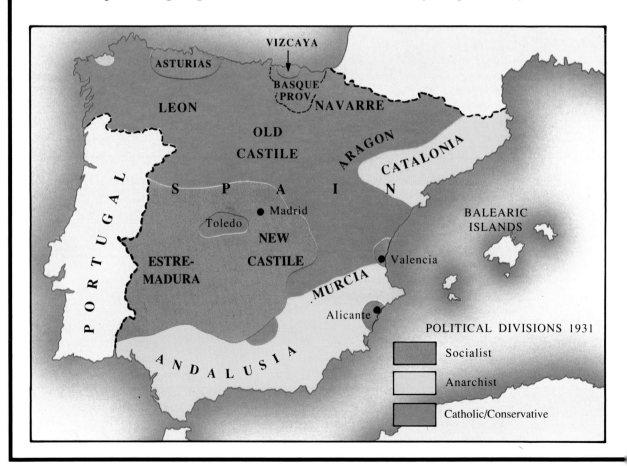

POLITICAL DIVISIONS 1931

Socialist

Anarchist

Catholic/Conservative

great estates. Among these poor peasants, anarchism became a powerful movement. Anarchists believed that the state should be abolished in favor of loosely organized, self-governing collectives. They were hostile to the Church, which they identified with their rich oppressors, and they dreamed of seizing the land for themselves.

Anarchism was also strong in the northeastern province of Catalonia, especially among the industrial workers of Barcelona, many of whom belonged to militant trade unions. The rival force of socialism was influential in Madrid and the coal-mining and industrial regions of Vizcaya and Asturias in the north.

Parliamentary democracy was opposed by various right-wing groups. The Church, with its traditional support, had its own political organizations. In Navarre, there was also a strong movement called the Carlists. They opposed the ruling king, Alfonso XIII, and supported the claim to the throne of the descendants of Don Carlos (1788–1855). They wanted to restore an absolute monarchy in the style of Spain's medieval rulers.

A further threat to democracy was represented by the army, which had a long tradition of interfering in politics. Between 1820 and 1923, there were forty-three army coups or *pronunciamientos* ("pronouncements"). Since 1923, Spain had been governed by a military dictator, General Miguel Primo de Rivera.

Spanish politics was also complicated by strong regional divisions. People in the Basque Provinces and Catalonia had their own languages and distinctive cultures and wanted to separate from the rest of Spain.

The economic crisis following the Wall Street Crash brought down the dictatorship of Primo de Rivera and then the monarchy itself. In April 1931, after a massive electoral victory by the republican parties, King Alfonso abdicated. Spain became a Republic. The new government tried to modernize Spain, taking over some of the biggest estates and reducing the powers of the Church. This attack on religion and private property mobilized opposition. In the 1936 election, Spain split into two political "fronts." Liberals, communists, socialists, republicans and anarchists formed the Popular Front; conservatives, monarchists (Alfonsist and Carlist) and the Catholic CEDA Party formed the National Front, supported by the army and the Church. The Popular Front won a narrow victory – 4.2 million votes against the Nationalists' 3.8 million. The defeated Nationalists plotted to seize power.

◀ The political map of Spain in 1931, the year the Republic was proclaimed. Five years later these political divisions would lead to civil war.

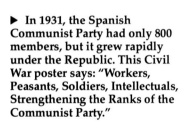

▶ In 1931, the Spanish Communist Party had only 800 members, but it grew rapidly under the Republic. This Civil War poster says: "Workers, Peasants, Soldiers, Intellectuals, Strengthening the Ranks of the Communist Party."

The Falange

José Antonio Primo de Rivera, the young lawyer who founded the Falange. Like other fascists, he was anti-democratic and feared the spread of communism. But he was equally hostile to capitalism, which he blamed for the poverty of Spain's landless peasants. Unlike Hitler and Mussolini, José Antonio was an upper-class intellectual who never felt completely comfortable in the role of fascist leader.

In 1931, two young Spaniards, Ramiro Ledesma Ramos and Onésimo Redondo Ortega, founded Spain's first fascist party. It was called the *Juntas de Ofensiva Nacional Syndicalista* (Groups of National Syndicalist Offensive) or JONS. It called for imperialist expansion, the abolition of democracy and state control of the economy; employers and workers were to be organized in national syndicates. The JONS was to be a revolutionary movement inspired by Spain's glorious imperial past. It attracted a small following among students, disillusioned anarchists, taxi drivers and waiters. But its program had little mass appeal.

In 1933, José Antonio Primo de Rivera, the son of the deposed dictator founded a second fascist party, the *Falange Española* (Spanish Phalanx; the word "phalanx" means "line of battle"). At a meeting in Madrid, de Rivera explained the political principles of the Falange Party:

> *It belongs, this must be stated clearly once and for all, neither to the Right nor to the Left. On the Right there is the intention to maintain an economic order that is unjust. On the Left there is the idea to overthrow the economic order, even if this means losing much that is good . . . We struggle for a totalitarian state that will distribute its fruits fairly to the small and to the big people.*[28]

In Spain in the 1930s such a program lacked a strong, broad base.

Like the JONS, the Falange combined revolutionary aims with the belief in a Catholic, imperial Spain, founded on authority and order. In 1934, the two parties merged under José Antonio's leadership. The new Falange took the flag of the JONS and Ledesma's slogan, *"Arriba! España, Una, Grande, Libre!"* ("Arise! Spain, One, Great, Free!"). Its members wore blue shirts and adopted the fascist salute.

The Falange won strong support only from students. The majority of its 8,000 members in 1935 were under twenty-one and too young to vote. Spain lacked the social groups that could have provided a mass base for fascism. The country had not taken part in World War I, so there were no discontented war veterans.

The lower middle classes, which had supported fascism in Italy and Germany, were much less numerous in Spain.

Unable to win elections, the Falangists relied increasingly on violence. They fought in the streets with socialist and communist youth groups, and they assassinated opponents. In March 1936, the Popular Front government arrested José Antonio and outlawed his party. It would take the Spanish Civil War to turn the Falange into a mass movement, but by the time war broke out, the radical leaders of the Falange were almost all in Republican prisons.

▼(Left) A Civil War painting of a Falange militiaman.

▼(Right) A poster showing a Falangist youth sweeping Spain free of evil elements, including communism, anarchism and social injustice.

Civil War

Throughout the spring and early summer of 1936, the Nationalists plotted to rise against the Popular Front government. An excuse for the rising was provided on July 13, when the monarchist leader, José Calvo Sotelo, was murdered by members of the state police. Four days later there was a rebellion of the Spanish army in Morocco. The army also rebelled on the Spanish mainland in Navarre, led by General Mola and supported by the Carlists.

On July 22, General Franco, leader of the Moroccan forces, announced:

> *The movement we are proclaiming has nothing in common with petty politics; it is a nationalist Spanish movement with the sole aim of saving Spain.*[29]

But what was Spain to be saved from?

The Nationalist rebels included groups with many different political aims: conservatives, Carlists and Falangists. Franco was deliberately vague about his long-term objectives. He drew on the different groups' common Catholicism, presenting the rising as a defensive religious crusade against godless communism. As the only Nationalist leader who was not linked with any particular faction, Franco was able to take overall control of the rising.

The Republican side was more divided over its war aims and never able to unite in the same way. The extreme left wanted to create a revolutionary workers' state. Anarchists and left-wing socialists seized the land, occupied the factories and set up workers' militias. But the Liberals wanted only to save democracy. They were supported by the Spanish Communist Party, which took its orders from Moscow. The Communists argued that the workers' revolution would split the Popular Front and lead to Franco's victory. As the Republic increasingly depended on armaments from the USSR, the Soviet leader Stalin was able to influence Popular Front policy. In May 1937, these divisions led to open fighting between the pro-Stalin Communists and the POUM, a

Franco's troops enter Madrid in triumph. The fall of Spain's capital city in March 1939 marked the end of the Civil War.

communist party that supported Stalin's rival, Trotsky. The POUM was outlawed and its leaders shot.

Franco received important military aid from Italy and Germany. But the Republic received no support from fellow democracies. Individual socialists did go to fight against the Nationalists, but the British Conservative government feared the spread of communism far more than fascism; it even put pressure on France to ban arms sales to the Republic. It did set up a Non-Intervention Committee to prevent foreign interference in the conflict, but it was ignored by Hitler and Mussolini.

Besides being better armed, Franco's forces were much more disciplined than the Republican forces. The Popular Front Army depended on workers' militias, which elected their own officers and discussed strategy at length. They were democratic, but lacked vital speed and efficiency. In contrast, the Nationalists had thousands of trained officers under centralized control. Franco was a cautious general who would not launch an offensive without thorough preparation. Slowly and systematically, the Nationalists won the war.

► (Above) A Republican poster issued by the socialist Union of General Workers. The soldier says, "I go to fight for your future."

► (Below) The Republican prime minister, Largo Caballero, surrounded by the different elements of the Popular Front – communists, anarchists and republicans. Despite this appearance of unity, these groups often hated each other as much as they hated Franco.

Franco and fascism

After his arrest, José Antonio Primo de Rivera had continued to direct the Falange from prison. He gave his support to the military rising against the Republic, but warned his followers:

> *I fear . . . the establishment of a false, conservative Fascism without revolutionary courage and young blood.*[30]

In November 1936, José Antonio was put on trial for conspiring against the Republic and executed. His death provided the Nationalists with an official martyr, but left the Falange leaderless. It could now be taken over by Franco. The general had little sympathy with the radical ideas of the Falange, but saw the movement as a way of mobilizing Spain's idealistic youth and winning support from the foreign fascist regimes. The Falange was given control of the Nationalist propaganda and it proclaimed the fight for "the fatherland, bread and justice." In the Nationalist areas of the country, thousands volunteered for the party's militia, and for the first time it became a mass movement.

That the Falange had no real political role was demonstrated in April 1937. Franco

At the end of the Civil War, José Antonio Primo de Rivera's body was carried in a twenty-four hour procession from Alicante to El Escorial, where he was given a state funeral. Alive, José Antonio would have been a rival to Franco, and would have opposed his system. But dead, he became the official martyr of Franco's Spain.

Franco reviewing the army twenty-five years after his victory in the Civil War.

decreed that it should be united with the Carlists to form the new *Falange Tradicionalista y de las JONS*. It would be the official party of the new regime with Franco as its leader. Manuel Hedilla, the remaining Falangist leader, objected; his radical party had little in common with the monarchist Carlists. He was arrested and spent years in solitary confinement. Many of José Antonio's supporters saw Franco as a traitor to their movement and talked of "the lost Falange."[31]

After Franco had won the Civil War, he distanced himself from the foreign fascists, and in 1940 refused Hitler's request to bring Spain into World War II. Unlike Hitler and Mussolini, he did not want to conquer a new empire, and his cautious foreign policy

allowed his regime to survive until his death in 1975.

Franco's dictatorship shared some of the characteristics of the fascist regimes: he suppressed dissent, banned political parties, and replaced free trade unions with government-controlled labor syndicates. But unlike the Führer and the Duce, Franco did not depend on the support of a mass party, and he did not demand popular enthusiasm for his regime. He needed only passive acceptance from the Spanish. His rule benefited Spain's traditional ruling classes, the rich landowners and the Church.

5
VARIETIES OF FASCISM
The British Union of Fascists

DURING THE ECONOMIC DEPRESSION of the 1930s, fascist-style parties appeared throughout Europe. Among them were the Belgian Rexists, the Finnish Lapua movement, the Fiery Cross and the Popular Party in France, and the Hungarian Arrow Cross. Yet none of the groups was able to repeat the success of Hitler and Mussolini. To understand why fascism failed outside Germany and Italy, we shall look at some specific examples – Britain, Denmark, Norway and Romania.

In 1930 the world depression caused British unemployment to rise to over two million. Oswald Mosley, a junior minister in the Labor government, called for a massive increase in public spending to solve the problem. The government, unwilling to increase the national debt, rejected Mosley's plan and he resigned. He began to talk about a new political movement. It would represent the "revolt of the young manhood of Britain" against "the Old Gang of our present political system."[32] It would go beyond class differences and rally all patriotic Britons.

Inspired by the example of Mussolini, Mosley set up the British Union of Fascists (BUF) in 1932. From Italy, he took the black shirts and the fascist salute. He began to hold mass rallies, theatrically staged in imitation of the Nazis. He tried to build a patriotic party in Britain modeled on very un-British foreign movements.

By the end of 1933, the BUF had 5,000 members. Mosley also received the support of an influential newspaper owner, Lord Rothermere. But despite a promising start, the BUF failed to win significant mass support. Mosley made a number of serious tactical mistakes.

Like the SA, the British blackshirts used violence, beating up hecklers at meetings.

After one notoriously violent rally in west London, Mosley lost the support of Rothermere. Influenced by Hitler, the BUF also began to adopt anti-Semitic policies. In London's East End, with its large Jewish immigrant population, anti-Semitism won working-class support. But the violence caused when the BUF marched through Jewish areas shocked middle-class followers. The government also responded, by passing a Public Order Act, banning marches and the wearing of uniforms.

Oswald Mosley gives the fascist salute. To many British people his black shirt looked suspiciously like the Italian uniform.

In July 1937, Mosley held a mass rally of fascists in Trafalgar Square in London. In the foreground anti-fascists give a clenched fist salute.

Although Mosley was unpopular because of his violent tactics, there were a number of other reasons why fascism attracted little support in Britain:

- The economic depression was much less severe in Britain than in Germany. There was no high inflation and, after 1933, the economy slowly recovered.
- Britain had been on the winning side in World War I and still had a large empire. There was no sense of frustrated nationalism.

- There was no "communist threat" from the tiny British Communist Party. Many working-class people supported the democratic Labor Party.
- The British political system was far more stable than those in Italy and Germany. Democratic institutions were widely unpopular in those countries, and seemed not to have been successful. By contrast, most British people accepted Parliament as the legitimate form of government.

When Britain went to war in 1939, Mosley was arrested as a security risk. The British Union of Fascists swiftly collapsed.

Scandinavian fascism

Overweight and undynamic, Fritz Clausen's lack of charisma was a major handicap for a fascist leader.

Scandinavian fascism was directly inspired by German Nazism. The Danish National Socialist Workers' Party (DNSAP) was founded in 1930, shortly after Hitler's success in the Reichstag elections. It was led by Fritz Clausen. Hoping to get the same results by the same methods, the DNSAP copied both the program and the style of the Nazis: the swastika, the paramilitary SA and even the Nazi marching songs, which were translated into Danish. After Hitler came to power in 1933, Vidkun Quisling also founded Norway's *Nasjonal Samling* (National Unity) Party. Quisling copied Germany less than the DNSAP and used medieval Norse greetings and symbols. His central idea was the "Nordic Principle":

> *The Nordic Principle rests on Nordic traditions, Nordic thought and constructive cooperation, in contrast to Jewish liberalism and Marxism, which promote their destructive purposes by means of hatred, envy and class war.*[33]

Hitler would have agreed with all of this.

In the economic depression of the early 1930s, both parties attracted a few thousand members. But neither was able to win mass electoral support. In 1933, Quisling polled 2.2 percent of the vote, and in 1935 only 0.4 percent. The DNSAP polled 1 percent in 1935 and never managed to elect more than three members of parliament.

For a number of reasons, fascism failed completely in Scandinavia. Denmark had only 6,000, well-integrated Jews, Norway less than 2,000, so anti-Semitism had little appeal. It was further discredited as the news of Nazi brutality against the Jews spread. Neither Norway nor Denmark had taken part in World War I, and neither country had territorial grievances. There were no discontented war veterans who might provide initial support for fascism. The communist threat was also absent.

In both Scandinavian countries, the party political system did not leave any space where a fascist party could grow. Denmark's parties met the needs of all the country's social groups and provided stable government. In Norway a period of instability ended in 1935, when the Labor Party and the Agrarian Party formed a

▲ Norwegian fascists on the march.

coalition government. In contrast to Italy and Germany, none of the established parties was willing to form alliances with the fascists.

Quisling and Clausen were caught up in the same contradiction as Mosley. They claimed to be nationalists, yet they were closely identified with a powerful foreign nation. The German connection was especially damaging in Denmark, which had lost territory to Germany in 1864 and was traditionally anti-German. By the start of World War II in 1939, Scandinavian fascists were completely discredited.

In 1940, Germany invaded Denmark and Norway, occupying both countries until 1945. Nazi occupation gave the Scandinavian fascists an artificial lease of life. But they could no longer present themselves convincingly as nationalists. They collaborated with the German invaders, and the name "Quisling" even entered the English language as a new word for "traitor."

◀ Vidkun Quisling claimed that he was not a fascist but a Norwegian nationalist. His party, National Unity, looked back to the greatness of Viking Norway as its model.

Romania: peasant fascism

At the end of World War I, Romania had been among the winning nations. After the peace treaties, the country doubled in size. With the newly-gained lands came large numbers of foreigners: Hungarians, Ukrainians and Yiddish-speaking Jews.

Romania had a long history of anti-Semitism. Most Romanians were peasants, or the children of peasants. Jews had formed a large part of the country's tiny middle class. Traditionally they had acted as middlemen, tax collectors and estate managers employed by wealthy landlords. They were an

Unlike Germany, Romania's problems resulted from *gaining* territory in the 1919 peace treaties. Romanians felt threatened by the influx of Jews and foreigners.

obvious focus for the resentment of the poor peasantry.

Communism had little influence, for it was identified with Romania's neighbor and traditional enemy, Russia. Many communist leaders were Jewish, so communism could also be identified with the Jews. For these reasons, Romanian nationalism was closely linked with hatred of communists and Jews.

In 1927, a group of students led by Corneliu Codreanu founded the Legion of the Archangel Michael, a religious, nationalistic organization, hostile to democracy, communism and the Jews. The Legion was not to be a political party; in Codreanu's words, its task was "not to formulate programs, but to create men, a new kind

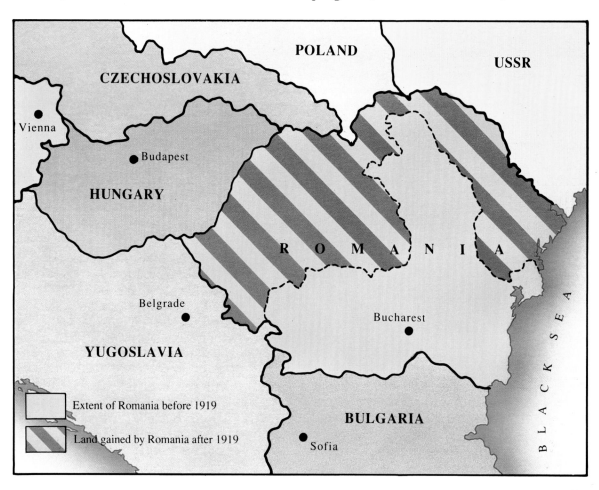

Extent of Romania before 1919

Land gained by Romania after 1919

King Carol hated the democratic system and, in February 1938, declared himself dictator. He banned all political parties and had the Legion's leader, Codreanu, arrested. Carol set up his own party, the Front of National Revival, complete with military uniforms and a youth section. But his dictatorship lasted little more than two years. In September 1940 Carol was forced to abdicate by the army, which set up a military dictatorship under General Antonescu.

of man!"[34] The Legionaries wore green shirts, symbolizing the "spring of the Romanian nation."[35] They traveled to remote villages, and they worked in the fields with peasants who had been ignored by the traditional parties. Codreanu described a 1930 journey through Bessarabia, a region with a high proportion of Jews:

> *Singing we rode through the streets: "Romanians awake, awake!" . . . On our breasts the white linen crosses glowed. We looked like crusaders. And crusaders we wanted to be, knights who in the name of the cross were fighting the godless Jewish powers to liberate Romania.*[36]

The religious peasants responded with fervor to the appearance of Codreanu.

Codreanu himself inspired fanatical loyalty in his followers. Believing they were fighting a religious battle against evil, the Legionaries were ready to kill or be killed for

their cause. By 1937, they had murdered several important politicians. Codreanu also contested elections, increasing his support from 34,000 votes (1.2 percent) in 1931 to 478,000 votes (16 percent) in 1937. With sixty-six parliamentary seats, his party was the third strongest in Romania.

Success was brief. Romania's King Carol shared Codreanu's hatred of democracy, but felt threatened by the Legion's growing electoral appeal. Supported by Romania's industrialists, the army and police force, in February 1938 Carol declared himself dictator. Thousands of Legionaries were arrested. In November, Codreanu and thirteen followers were strangled by their guards. It was announced that they had been "shot while trying to escape."

After Codreanu's death, the Legion continued to have some political influence, but in 1941 it was finally crushed by the Romanian army under a new military dictator, General Antonescu.

6
INTERPRETATIONS
Fascism and big business

SINCE MUSSOLINI first attracted international attention in the 1920s, political theorists have attempted to explain the significance of fascism. Some claim that fascism as a single phenomenon does not exist, but that the fascist movements were each particular results of individual national problems. Others have described fascism as a kind of "moral disease"[37] affecting a Europe torn apart by World War I, or a form of "war psychosis,"[38] which drew people toward irrational movements promising order and salvation.

From the start, the interpretation of fascism posed a particular problem for the communists. The *Communist Manifesto* of Karl Marx and Friedrich Engels explained that society had split "into two great hostile camps,"[39] the capitalist bourgeoisie and the working classes, and that the victory of the latter was inevitable. The question was, which camp did the fascists belong to? Was fascism a revolutionary movement, as it claimed, or was it really just an instrument of big business? The Program of the 1928 Communist International provided an answer:

> *In periods of acute crisis for the bourgeois, fascism resorts to anti-capitalist phraseology, but, after it has established itself at the helm of the state, it casts aside its anti-capitalist rattle and discloses itself as a terrorist dictatorship of big capital.[40]*

Hitler meets German businessmen in 1933. He needed their money to pay for Nazi election campaigns. They hoped the Nazis would further their business interests.

Communists were unwilling to admit that any other ideology bore the true revolutionary stamp. There was some truth in their claims.

During the struggle for power, both Hitler and Mussolini did use "anti-capitalist phraseology." Yet after they had taken over, they both suppressed their revolutionary followers. Communists were also right to point out that fascist economic policies – the drive to self-sufficiency, massive rearmament and the banning of trade unions – all benefited heavy industry.

In return, big business did give important financial support to the fascists. However, most historians now agree that big business did not really control fascism. Like the right-wing politicians, some financiers mistakenly thought they could use fascism as a tool to destroy communism, and then "tame" it. Fritz Thyssen was one important industrialist who gave enormous sums to the Nazis, but broke with them when he realized that Hitler was leading Germany into a disastrous war. In his 1941 book, *I Paid Hitler*, Thyssen wrote:

> *I believed that by backing Hitler and his party I could contribute to the reinstatement of real government and of orderly conditions, which would enable all branches of activity – and especially business – to function normally once again . . . In fact, the Nazi regime has ruined German industry.*[41]

Historians have also shown that some German industrialists only gave significant support to fascism once it had already become a popular movement. Capitalist support did indeed help Hitler and Mussolini to seize power, but on its own it does not fully explain the rise of fascism as a mass movement.

▲ Communist propaganda presented fascism as a tool of big business. This photomontage, "The meaning of the Hitler salute," is by John Heartfield, a Czech artist. He gave a new meaning to Hitler's boast, "Millions stand behind me."

◄ A communist painting showing the international working class united and advancing toward the socialist future. To capitalists such an image was both disturbing and threatening.

Who were the fascists?

Another way of interpreting fascism is to look at the type of people who joined the fascist parties or voted for them.

Fascism seems to have had a particular appeal to youth. Compared with the traditional political leaders of Europe, the fascist leaders were all young men. In 1933, Hitler was 44, Mussolini 50, Mosley 37, Codreanu 31 and Primo de Rivera 30. They all glorified youth, praising its energy and appealing to the idealism of self-sacrifice and patriotism. Mussolini's national anthem was even called "Youth" ("*Giovinezza*"). Fascism

A mass salute by the Hitler Youth. Fascism made a strong emotional appeal to the young.

can be explained, in part, as a rebellion of the young against what Mosley scathingly called "the Old Gang."[42]

Fascism also claimed to be a movement that could appeal across class barriers in the higher interests of the nation. However, electoral figures show that neither Hitler nor Mussolini won substantial support from the working classes; they remained loyal to the socialist or Catholic parties. Most historians agree that the Nazis and the Italian Fascists drew their greatest support from the lower middle classes – shopkeepers, small businessmen, farmers and office workers. There are several reasons why this normally moderate group was attracted to fascism.

Nazi propaganda aimed at owners of small shops. The Jewish department-store octopus devours the small shops. A large part of Hitler's support came from the lower middle classes.

As early as 1923, the Italian historian Luigi Salvatorelli wrote that Italian fascism represented the class struggle of the middle classes, trapped between big business and the workers, "like a third man between two fighters."[43] Lacking the bargaining power of organized labor or the strength of big business, this was the group that had lost most in the economic crisis following World War I. Middle-class people also feared loss of status, of being leveled down into the working classes. Before 1919, the German middle classes had occupied a protected position within an authoritarian state. When the Weimar Republic gave political representation to the working classes, the middle classes lost their special status.

Unlike the traditional middle-class parties, fascism seemed to provide the solution to the economic crisis. It claimed to be hostile to both big business and trade unions. It offered a return to the traditional values of authority and obedience. The Nazi program promised the creation of a "healthy middle class."[44] Hitler promised to protect small businesses from the competition of the department stores.

However, the example of Romania shows that fascism can attract mass support in other social groups. The important thing is for a sufficiently large section of society to be discontented with the system. Where this was not the case, as in Britain and Scandinavia, fascism failed. Fascism has been described as a "mass movement of the discontented,"[45] appealing to those uprooted by war, under threat from social change or unrepresented by the existing parties.

Leading figures

Codreanu, Corneliu Zelea (1899–1938), leader of Romania's Legion of the Archangel Michael.

Born in a part of Romania with a high proportion of Jews, Codreanu was brought up as a fanatical anti-Semite and nationalist. At the University of Jasi, he came under the influence of Professor A. C. Cuza and his "League of Christian and National Defense," an anti-Semitic organization with the swastika as its emblem. For a while, he worked with the League, beating up Jews and political opponents. In 1923, while briefly imprisoned for having threatened to shoot "traitors," he was struck by an image of St. Michael, the warrior archangel. This image inspired his formation, in 1927, of the Legion of the Archangel Michael, a student order aiming to save Romania from communism and the Jews. The Legion had more in common with a religious cult than with a political party. Fascinated by death, the Legionaries sang songs in which they welcomed the prospect of martyrdom. They were ready to kill or die for Codreanu, whom they called "the Captain."

In 1930, Codreanu set up the "Iron Guard," a mass movement to fight elections. Romania's other political parties had ignored the peasantry, but the Legionaries campaigned in remote villages, working with the peasants and teaching them their songs. Between 1931 and 1937, the Iron Guard increased its vote from 1.2 to 16 percent. However, in February 1938, when King Carol declared himself dictator, Codreanu was arrested and charged with conspiracy and treason. In November, he was strangled by his police escort. To the Legionaries, their dead Captain was a holy martyr. The following September, they avenged him by assassinating King Carol's chief minister, Calinescu. The cycle of Legionary murders and government reprisals escalated during 1939, called the "year of martyrdom" by Codreanu's followers. Following a brief Legionary uprising in 1941, the movement was finally suppressed by the army.

Franco, Francisco (1892–1975), Spanish general and Caudillo (leader).

Franco came from a military family in Galicia and made his reputation as commander of the Spanish Foreign Legion in Morocco. In 1934, he directed the brutal suppression of a left-wing rising by Asturian miners, arousing the distrust of Spain's left-wing politicians. When they won the February 1936 election, they exiled Franco to command Spain's forces in the Canary Islands. There he was persuaded by his fellow generals to join a conspiracy against the Republic. Unlike the other generals, Franco was not identified with a particular faction in the rising. His ability to win support from all the nationalist groups made him overall leader. Franco made use of fascism to mobilize support from Spain's youth and to win backing from Mussolini and Hitler. But once he had won the civil war, he appeared in his true colors as an old-fashioned conservative.

Francisco Franco, military dictator of Spain from 1939 to 1975.

Hitler, Adolf (1889–1945), Führer (leader) of Nazi Germany.

Hitler was the son of an Austrian customs official and grew up on the German border. He spent years drifting among the down-and-outs of Vienna, with vague hopes of becoming an artist. The outbreak of World War I in 1914 gave him a sense of purpose. Hitler volunteered for a Bavarian infantry regiment and spent the war years on the Western Front, where his bravery won him the Iron Cross. The army, with its masculine comradeship and its regimented life, had a deep effect on Hitler's character. In 1918, he was devastated by the news of Germany's surrender. He believed that the army had not been defeated but stabbed in the back by Jews and communists.

After the war, he continued to work for the army as a propaganda officer, countering the spread of communist ideas among the soldiers. This work brought him into contact with the tiny German Workers' Party, later to become the Nazi Party. With his forceful personality, he soon became the leader of the party and led its failed attempt to seize power in 1923. Hitler then spent nine months in prison writing *Mein Kampf*, a mixture of autobiography and political philosophy. Its central theme is racial conflict. Hitler believed that all human culture had been created by the so-called Aryan race, represented by the Germans, and that Jews posed a threat to civilization by their existence. Germans had a duty to remain racially pure and a right to conquer other races for "living space." When *Mein Kampf* was published, it was largely dismissed as the ravings of a fanatic. But these were the ideas that Hitler put into practice after he became Führer in 1933. His aggressive foreign policy led to the outbreak of World War II in September 1939. In April 1945, when it was obvious that Germany had lost the war, Hitler shot himself.

Hitler in 1936.

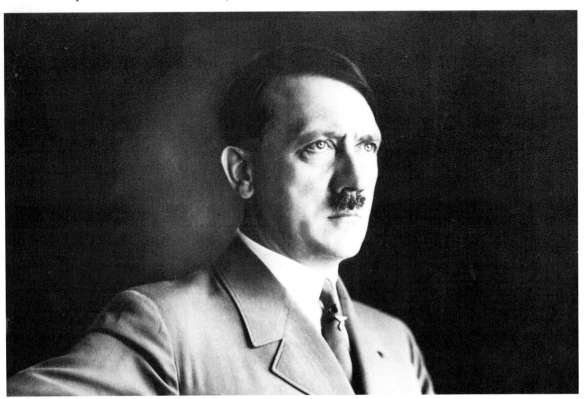

Sir Oswald Mosley saluting his followers on a British Union of Fascists march.

Mosley, Sir Oswald (1896–1980), leader of the British Union of Fascists.

Mosley came from an aristocratic Staffordshire family and served in the trenches in World War I. He was invalided out in 1916 and went into politics, becoming a Conservative Member of Parliament at the age of twenty-one. Gradually he grew disenchanted with the Conservatives and joined the Labor Party.

In 1929, Mosely was given a junior cabinet position in Britain's first Labor government. His special responsibility was unemployment, which rose rapidly under the impact of the Wall Street Crash. Mosley's solution, a massive program of public spending, was rejected and he resigned. His experiences as a Member of Parliament in both major parties convinced him that party politics could not solve Britain's problems. What was needed was to sweep out the "Old Gang" who ran Britain and find something new. Mosley found what he was looking for in Fascist Italy.

In 1932, Mosley founded the British Union of Fascists (BUF). Its aim was to set up an authoritarian corporate state on the Italian model. The BUF adopted black shirts and the Fascist salute. In the mid-1930s, Mosley was increasingly influenced by Hitler, even adopting anti-Semitic policies. They were popular among some working-class people in London's East End, but anti-Semitism worried his middle-class followers, as did the violence that often took place at BUF rallies. Mosley was a charismatic speaker, but he never managed to attract mass support. At the outbreak of World War II, he was arrested as a security risk and the BUF collapsed. His attempts to revive fascism after the war also failed.

Mussolini, Benito (1883–1945), Duce (leader) of Italy.

Mussolini's father was a blacksmith and his mother a teacher. He grew up in the Romagna, a region of Italy with strong socialist traditions. He first came to public attention as a socialist journalist, editing the party newspaper, *Avanti!* But he was expelled from the party following his campaign for Italy's entry into World War I. Mussolini spent a few months at the front and was wounded. At the end of the war it seemed that Italy might undergo a communist revolution. As a nationalist, Mussolini was deeply opposed to communism, and in 1919 he formed the *Fasci di Combattimento*, a revolutionary movement that was also nationalistic.

Between 1919 and 1922, Italy was in a state of virtual anarchy. Increasingly, the Fascists seemed the only force strong enough to stop a left-wing revolution, and in October 1922, following the "march on Rome," Mussolini was appointed prime minister. Within three years, Italy was a dictatorship.

Mussolini's ambition was to restore the glory of ancient Rome. Through education and propaganda, he tried to turn the Italians into a fierce military nation. His dream of building a new Roman Empire led to Italy's invasion of Ethiopia in 1935, and an alliance with Hitler in World War II. At first, Mussolini had looked down on Hitler, but he was increasingly dominated by the German dictator. He began to copy the Nazis, introducing the goose step into the army. More sinisterly, he started an anti-Jewish campaign, although many Italians ignored his anti-Semitic laws.

In 1943, following the Allied conquest of Sicily, Mussolini was deposed by the Fascist Grand Council and the king. He was rescued by the Germans, who set up a fascist republic in the north of Italy. In the spring of 1945, when the Germans were in full retreat, Mussolini was captured and shot by Italian communist partisans. His body was strung up in Milan, mocked and abused by the people.

Quisling, Vidkun (1887–1945) Leader of Norway's *Nasjonal Samling* (National Unity) Party.

Vidkun Quisling had a military career before he entered politics. After studying at the Norwegian Military Academy, he spent several years in the USSR, working with the famous explorer Fridtjof Nansen in Russian relief work. Back in Norway he was invited to join the Agrarian Party government as minister of defense. Quisling served as a minister from 1931 to 1933, gaining notoriety for his suppression of a strike. In May 1933, he founded the *Nasjonal Samling* Party, inspired by the Nazi takeover of power in Germany. Quisling denied any connection with a foreign party and claimed that *Nasjonal Samling* was an attempt to revive the greatness of Viking Norway. However, unable to win elections, Quisling asked Hitler to help him seize power.

Following the German invasion in 1940, Quisling was made head of a puppet government. Held responsible for sending a thousand Jews to their deaths in Nazi concentration camps, in 1945 he was shot for treason.

Primo de Rivera, José Antonio (1903-36), founder of the Spanish Falange.

José Antonio was the son of General Miguel Primo de Rivera, the dictator of Spain from 1923 to 1930. After studying law, he entered politics, his major aim being to defend the reputation of his father. He rejected the injustices of the capitalist system but, as a Catholic and a patriot, he was equally hostile to communism. In October 1933, he set up the *Falange Española*, a fascist party supported mainly by students. In March 1936, following increasing Falangist violence, the Popular Front government arrested José Antonio and outlawed the Falange. He continued to direct the movement from prison, warning his followers to remain independent of the conservative military leaders. After the army rose against the Republic, he was tried for helping to prepare the revolt. In November 1936, José Antonio was shot in Alicante. His death made him a Nationalist martyr.

Important dates

Date	Events
1914–18	World War I.
1918	*November 9* German Kaiser abdicates. Weimar Republic is proclaimed. *November 11* The armistice is signed.
1919	*March 23* Mussolini founds *Fasci di Combattimento* in Milan. *June 28* Treaty of Versailles signed. *September 12* D'Annunzio occupies Fiume. *September 16* Hitler joins the German Workers' Party in Munich.
1921	*July 29* Hitler elected chairman of the Nazi Party.
1922	*October 28* Mussolini's march on Rome.
1923	*January 11* Following the German failure to pay reparations, French troops occupy the Ruhr. *September 13* Military coup in Spain by General Primo de Rivera. *November 8–9* Hitler's attempt to seize power in Munich (the Munich *Putsch*).
1924	*April 1* Hitler sentenced to five years' imprisonment. *June 10* Socialist deputy Matteotti kidnapped and murdered by blackshirts. *December 20* Hitler released under a general amnesty.
1925	*January 3* Mussolini assumes the powers of a dictator. *February 27* The Nazi Party refounded.
1927	*June* Codreanu founds Romania's Legion of the Archangel Michael.
1929	*February 11* Mussolini's Lateran Pacts with the Roman Catholic Church. *October 29* The Wall Street Crash.
1930	*January* General Primo de Rivera dismissed by King Alfonso XIII of Spain. *May 21* Oswald Mosley resigns from the Labor government. *September 14* Nazis win 107 seats in the Reichstag elections. *November* Denmark's National Socialist Workers' Party founded.
1931	*April 14* King Alfonso goes into exile. Spain becomes a Republic.
1932	*July 31* Nazis win 230 seats in the Reichstag elections.

Date	Events
	October 1 Mosley founds the British Union of Fascists.
1933	*January 30* Hitler appointed chancellor of Germany.
	March 23 Enabling Law gives Hitler the right to govern by decree.
	May 17 Vidkun Quisling founds Norway's *Nasjonal Samling*.
	October 29 The *Falange Española* founded under the leadership of José Antonio Primo de Rivera.
1934	*June 29–30* Purge of the SA in the "Night of the Long Knives."
1936	*February 16* Popular Front wins Spanish elections.
	March 14 Falange outlawed and its leaders are arrested.
	July Start of the Spanish Civil War.
	November 20 José Antonio Primo de Rivera executed in Alicante.
	December British government passes a Public Order Act to curb the activities of the British Union of Fascists.
1937	*April 19* Franco unites the Falange with other right-wing groups to form the *Falange Española Tradicionalista*.
	December Codreanu gets 478,378 votes (16 percent) in the Romanian elections.
1938	*February* King Carol of Romania bans political parties. Codreanu arrested. Over the next year, more than 1,200 Legionaries, including Codreanu, are killed.
1939	*March–April* End of the Spanish Civil War.
	September 3 Outbreak of World War II.
1940	*April 9* Germany invades Denmark and Norway. Quisling declares himself prime minister.
	June 10 Mussolini brings Italy into the war as Hitler's ally.
1945	*April 28* Mussolini shot by communist partisans.
	April 30 Hitler commits suicide.
	October 24 Quisling shot for treason.

Glossary

Anarchism	The belief that government by the state should be abolished.
Anti-Semitism	Hostility to Jewish people.
Assassination	The murder of a political figure, often for political reasons.
Authoritarian	Favoring obedience of authority over individual freedom.
Bolsheviks	The Russian Communist Party that seized power in 1917.
Bourgeois	Middle class. The term is often used by communists to refer to capitalists.
Capitalism	An economic system based on free enterprise and the private ownership of industry.
Caudillo	Spanish military or political leader. The title of Franco.
Chancellor	In Germany, the head of government.
Charisma	Ability to inspire followers with loyalty and devotion.
Communism	An economic and political theory. It is based on the abolition of private property, state control of industry and the creation of a classless society.
Conservatism	The belief that social institutions should be preserved. Hostility to reform or change in society.
Corporative state	A state that is governed by or organized in large bodies called corporations, especially of employers and employees.
Dictatorship	Absolute government, usually by one person.
Duce	The Italian leader, Mussolini.
Führer	The German leader, Hitler.
Inflation	Increase in the level of prices and fall in the value of money.
Internationalism	The belief in friendly cooperation among nations. Internationalism is also the specific socialist belief that the workers of all nations share common interests.

Imperialism	The policy of extending a country's rule over other territories.
Left wing	General term covering all political beliefs based on human equality and the need for radical social change: socialism, communism and anarchism. The most radical sections of European parliaments traditionally sat on the left of the presiding official.
Liberalism	The political belief that stresses individual freedom and parliamentary democracy.
Lock-out	An employer's method of forcing workers to accept his or her conditions by refusing them work or locking them out.
Nationalism	Feelings of patriotism and the desire to make one's country strong and independent.
Parliamentary democracy	Government by the people, through their elected representatives in parliament.
Republic	Form of government with an elected head of state instead of a monarch or dictator.
Right wing	General term covering the groups most hostile to left-wing ideas – conservatives, nationalists and monarchists. As extreme nationalists who believed in strong government, fascists are usually thought of as right wing. But the fascists themselves denied this.
Socialism	A political belief that stresses the principle of social equality, and calls for the redistribution of wealth and state control of the economy.
Soviet	Russian word for a council. Workers' and soldiers' soviets were set up to seize power in Russia in 1917 and Germany in 1918–19.
Syndicalism	A revolutionary trade union movement, named after the French word for trade union, *syndicat*. The syndicalists believed that workers' unions should seize power, by organizing a general strike.

Further reading

Easier Books

R. Herzstein, *The Nazis* (Silver, 1980)

Scholarly Books

Laquer, Walter (ed.) *Fascism: A Reader's Guide* (U. of Cal. Pr. , 1977)

Larsen, Stein U. *Who Were the Fascists? Social Roots of European Fascism* (Oxford U. Pr., 1981)

Lyttelton, Adrian *The Seizure of Power. Fascism in Italy 1919-29* (Princeton U. Pr., 1988)

Mosse, George L. *Masses & Man: Nationalist & Fascist Perceptions of Reality* (Wayne St. U. Pr., 1987)

Payne, Stanley G. *Fascism* (U. of Wis. Pr., 1980) Payne, Stanley G. *Falange: A History of Spanish Fascism* (Stanford U. Pr., 1961)

Notes on sources

1 Quoted by C. F. Delzell, *Mediterranean Fascism*, Macmillan, 1970, p 97.
2 *Ibid.*, p 42.
3 Quoted by G. Mann, *The History of Germany since 1789*, Penguin, 1974, p 717.
4 Quoted by E. Weber, *Varieties of Fascism*, Anvil, 1964, p 56.
5 Quoted by M. Gallo, *Mussolini's Italy*, Abelard-Schuman, 1973, p 53.
6 *Ibid.*, p 151.
7 Quoted by Delzell, *op. cit.*, p 40.
8 Quoted by L. Chabod *A History of Italian Fascism*, Howard Fertig, 1975, p 56.
9 Quoted by A. Lyttelton, "Fascism in Italy. The Second Wave" in *International Fascism*, ed. G. L. Mosse, Sage, 1979, p 63.
10 Quoted by Delzell, *op. cit.*, p 57.
11 Quoted by A. Lyttelton, *The Seizure of Power – Fascism in Italy 1919-29*, Weidenfeld & Nicolson, 1987, p 333.
12 Quoted by Gallo, *op. cit.*, p 235.
13 Quoted by Emil Ludwig, *Talks with Mussolini*, George Allen, 1932, p 122-3, p 128.
14 Quoted by Lyttelton, *op. cit.*, p 269.
15 Quoted by C. Hibbert, *Benito Mussolini*, Longmans, 1962, p 255.
16 Quoted by Gallo, *op. cit.*, p 224.
17 Quoted by D. Mack Smith, *Mussolini*, Weidenfeld & Nicolson, 1981, p 280.
18 *Ibid.*, p 130.
19 Quoted by J. Noakes and G. Pridham, *Documents on Nazism 1919-45*, Jonathan Cape, 1974, p 104.
20 Quoted by Mann, *op. cit.*, p 675.
21 Quoted by G. L. Mosse, *Nazi Culture*, Grosset and Dunlap, 1968, p 40.
22 Quoted by D. Welch (ed.), *Nazi Propaganda*, Croom Helm, 1983, p 5.
23 Quoted by D. J. K. Peukert, *Inside Nazi Germany*, Batsford, 1987, p 237.
24 A. Speer, *Inside the Third Reich*, Sphere, 1971, p 295.

25 Quoted by I. Kershaw, *The Nazi Dictatorship: Problems and Perspectives of Interpretation*, Edward Arnold, 1985, p 62.
26 *Ibid.*
27 G. Orwell, *Homage to Catalonia*, Penguin, 1962, p 46.
28 Quoted by F. L. Carsten, *The Rise of Fascism*, Batsford, 1980, p 198.
29 Quoted by H. Browne, *Spain's Civil War*, Longman, 1983, p 83.
30 Quoted by Carsten, *op. cit.*, p 201.
31 José Yglesias, *The Franco Years*, BobbsMerrill, 1977, p 142.
32 Quoted by Weber, *op. cit.*, p 171.
33 *Ibid.*, p 155.
34 Quoted by N. M. Nagy-Talavera, *The Green Shirts and the Others – A History of Fascism in Hungary and Rumania*, Hoover Institute Press, 1970, p 267.
35 *Ibid.*, p 273.
36 Quoted by Carsten, *op. cit.*, p 186.
37 Renzo De Felice, *Interpretations of Fascism*, Harvard University Press, 1977, p 14.
38 *Ibid.*, p 111.
39 K. Marx and F. Engels, *Manifesto of the Communist Party* Progress, 1977, p 36.
40 Quoted by Weber, *op. cit.*, p 147.
41 F. Thyssen, *I Paid Hitler*, Farrar and Rinehart, 1941, p 32 and p 315.
42 Quotedd by Weber, *op. cit.*, p 171.
43 Quoted by B. Hagtvet and R. Kuhnl, "Contemporary Approaches to Fascism" in *Who Were the Fascists?* S. Larsen, B. Hagtvet and J. P. Mykleburst (eds.), Universitetsforlaget, 1980, p 29.
44 Quoted by L. L. Snyder (ed.), *Hitler's Third Reich. A Documentary Reader*, Nelson-Hall, 1981, p 24.
45 Otto-Ernst Schüddekopf, *Revolutions of Our Time. Fascism*, Weidenfeld & Nicolson, 1973, p 132.

Index

Figures in **bold** refer to illustrations

Picture acknowledgments

The author and publishers would like to thank the following for allowing their illustrations to be used in this book: E. T. Archive 21 (right), 39 (bottom); Mary Evans Picture Library *cover*, 6 (right); Hulton Picture Company 5, 16, 40; Peter Newark's Military Pictures 11 (top), 18, 19, 30, 31, 32, 37 (right), 38, 52; Popperfoto 11 (right), 13 (right), 14, 15, 20, 21 (top), 23 (right), 24, 41, 42, 47; Topham 4 (both), 6 (left), 7, 13, (left), 17, 36, 43, 44, 45 (left), 50, 54; Weimar Archive 12, 23, (top), 25, 26, 27, 28 (bottom), 33, 35, 37 (left), 39 (top), 45 (top), 48, 49, (both), 51. All other pictures are from the Wayland Picture Library. The artwork was supplied by Peter Bull.